♡

D0064576

For

_____,

An Officially Excellent Mom

_____

from

_____

date

OUR PURPOSE AT HOWARD PUBLISHING IS TO:

- *Increase faith* in the hearts of growing Christians
- *Inspire holiness* in the lives of believers
- *Instill hope* in the hearts of struggling people everywhere

BECAUSE HE'S COMING AGAIN!

The "Official" Mom Book © 2004 by Howard Publishing Co., Inc.
All rights reserved. Printed in the United States of America

Published by Howard Publishing Co., Inc.
3117 North 7th Street, West Monroe, Louisiana 71291-2227

04 05 06 07 08 09 10 11 12 13   10 9 8 7 6 5 4 3 2 1

Edited by Between the Lines
Interior design by Stephanie D. Walker
Illustrations by Kristy Caldwell
Cover design by LinDee Loveland

Library of Congress Cataloging-in-Publication Data
Bolton, Martha, 1951–
    The "official" mom book : the who, what, when, where, why, and how of motherhood /
Martha Bolton ; illustrated by Kristy Caldwell.
        p. cm.
    ISBN 1-58229-345-7 — ISBN 1-58229-346-5 (pbk.)
    1. Motherhood—Anecdotes. 2. Motherhood—Humor. I. Title.

HQ759.B638 2004
306.874'3—dc22   2003061847

Scripture quotations not otherwise marked are taken from the HOLY BIBLE, NEW INTERNATIONAL VERSION ®. Copyright © 1973, 1978, 1984 by International Bible Society. Used by permission of Zondervan. All rights reserved. Scriptures marked KJV are taken from the *Holy Bible*, Authorized King James Version.

"Mom's throughout History" was originally published in "The Cafeteria Lady," a column by Martha Bolton in *Brio* magazine, May 1996 and May 1997.

Every reasonable effort has been made to trace the ownership of quoted material. We will gladly make corrections in future editions provided that written notification is made to the publisher.

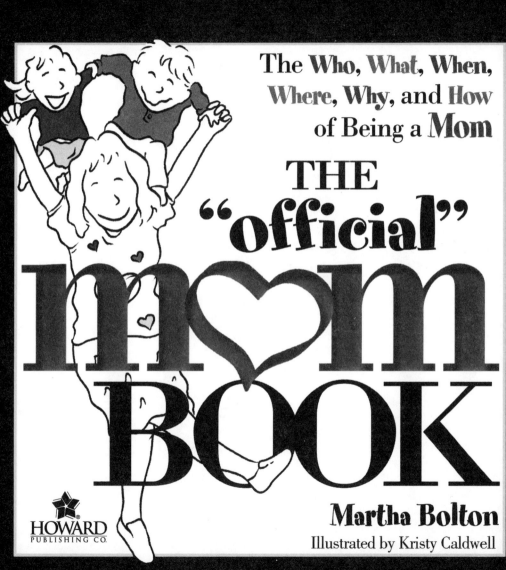

The **Who, What, When, Where, Why,** and **How** of Being a **Mom**

THE "official" m♥m BOOK

Martha Bolton

Illustrated by Kristy Caldwell

HOWARD
PUBLISHING CO.

Mom—where would we be
without you?

Dedication

To the memory of my own mother, Eunice, for her love, strength,
faith, and laughter. I cherish our time together.

To my other "mom," Diantha Ain, for her friendship,
encouragement, love, and wise counsel. You are a blessing to my life!

To my sons, Russ II, Matt, and Tony.
Thank you for the privilege of being called your mom. You were
a gift from God…even if you did all get here within two years!

To my daughters-in-law, Crystal and Nicole,
for the fun times we've shared. Glad you're in our family.

And to moms everywhere—where would any of us be without you?

Moms know what you're thinking, and they know what your teacher
wrote in the note you're hiding in your pocket.

Contents

Hurray for moms!

Mother's Day is in honor of the best Mother who ever lived—the Mother of your heart.

♡

Anna Jarvis

It's All about Mom

Moms. Everybody has one. In fact, the world is full of moms. Birth moms, adoptive moms, foster moms, moms-in-law, surrogate moms, rich moms, poor moms, middle-class moms. Moms of every age, shape, size, and nationality. Moms of all educational backgrounds, moms of every faith, famous moms and not-so-famous moms—everywhere you look, there are moms.

In 1914 President Woodrow Wilson thought so much of moms that he approved giving these special ladies their very own day. He proclaimed the second Sunday of May as Mother's Day in the United States, a tradition that continues to this day.

Moms also get songs written about them. And poetry. And books.

And movies. And according to florists, Mother's Day is always one of their highest grossing days, which means a lot of mothers are also getting flowers. Moms even get their own parking space at some grocery stores and shopping malls. You've probably seen the signs that say Reserved for Moms with Children or Reserved for Expectant Mothers.

So moms do get some recognition—just not nearly enough. That's why this book has been written. It's to further honor our moms. It's also to answer once and for all the who, what, when, where, why, and how of motherhood. Share it with a mother you love.

Flowers for you, Mom!

The mother's heart
is the child's schoolroom.

♥ Henry Ward Beecher ♥

Moms are in a class by themselves.

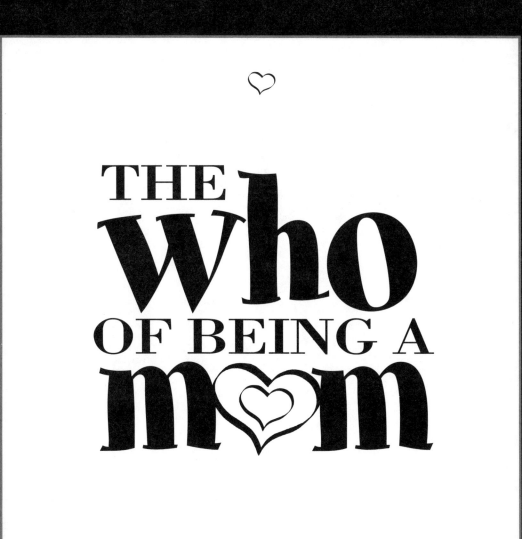

THE **who** OF BEING A **m♥m**

Who else would see us off to school in all kinds of weather?

Somehow even her clothes feel different to her children's hands from anybody else's clothes. Only to touch her skirt or her sleeve makes a troubled child feel better.

♡

Katherine Butler Hathaway

There's No One Like Mom

So who is this woman who thinks so much of us that she would stand on the corner in the rain, wearing reindeer slippers and Dad's overcoat just to make sure we get on the right school bus? Who is this lady who cheers the loudest during an awards ceremony because we won the Most Improved Student certificate—so loud you would think we'd just received the Nobel Peace Prize? Who is this unheralded chef who can make macaroni and cheese taste like a gourmet meal and who chauffeurs us to ball games, youth group meetings, and piano lessons, never once asking for a tip?

Mom, that's who. Whether you refer to her as Mom, Mother, Mommy, Ma, or Mama, one thing's for certain: These ladies are a class unto themselves.

A mother is the truest friend we have, when trials, heavy and sudden, fall upon us; when adversity takes the place of prosperity; when friends who rejoice with us in our sunshine, desert us when troubles thicken around us, still will she cling to us, and endeavor by her kind precepts and counsels to dissipate the clouds of darkness, and cause peace to return to our hearts.

❤ **Washington Irving** ❤

If your baby is beautiful
and perfect,
never cries or fusses,
sleeps on schedule
and burps on demand,
an angel all the time...
you're the grandma.

Teresa Bloomingdale

There was never a great man
who had not a great mother.

Oliver Schreiner

Giving Credit Where Credit's Due

Famous Sons Speak Out

My mother was the most beautiful woman I ever saw.

All I am I owe to my mother. I attribute all my success in life to the moral,

intellectual and physical education I received from her.

George Washington

There never was a woman like her. She was gentle as a dove and

brave as a lioness....The memory of my mother and her teachings were,

after all, the only capital I had to start life with,

and on that capital I have made my way.

Andrew Jackson

In all my efforts to learn to read, my mother shared fully my ambition and
sympathized with me and aided me in every way she could.
If I have done anything in life worth attention,
I feel sure that I inherited the disposition from my mother.

♥

Booker T. Washington

It seems to me that my mother was the
most splendid woman I ever knew....
I have met a lot of people
knocking around the world since,
but I have never met a more thoroughly
refined woman than my mother.
If I have amounted to anything,
it will be due to her.

♥

Charles Chaplin

My mother was the making of me. She was so true and so sure of me,
I felt that I had someone to live for—someone I must not disappoint.

♥

Thomas Edison

My mother's influence in molding my character was conspicuous.
She forced me to learn daily of chapters of the Bible by heart.
To that discipline and patient, accurate resolve I owe
not only much of my general power of taking pains,
but the best part of my taste for literature.

♥

John Ruskin

All that I am, or hope to be, I owe to my angel mother.

♥

Abraham Lincoln

I am eternally grateful to my mother for many things,
but one of the most enduring blessings she brought into my life
was to teach me the Catechism at the age of ten
that "God is Spirit, infinite, eternal, and unchangeable in his being,
wisdom, power, holiness, justice, goodness, and truth."
That definition of God has been with me all my life.

♥

Billy Graham

Men are what
their mothers made them.

♥

Ralph Waldo Emerson

Famous Daughters Speak Out

When Jimmy Carter was president, he called and said,
"Loretta, we want you to come up here. Five famous people will
come in and bring the teacher that has taught 'em the most."
…So, I told President Carter I couldn't bring a teacher. And he said,
"Why?" I said, "Well, my mommy was the one what taught me most."
And he said, "Well, there's always got to be a first. Bring her."
That was the biggest thrill that my mother ever had.

♥

Loretta Lynn

My mother wanted me to
be her wings,
to fly as she never quite
had the courage to do.

♥

Erica Jong

Momma was home.
She was the most totally human,
human being that I have ever known;
and so very beautiful.
She was the lighthouse of her community.
Within our home, she was an abundance
of love, discipline, fun, affection, strength,
tenderness, encouragement, understanding,
inspiration, and support.

Leontyne Price

Thanks to my mother, not a single cardboard box has
found its way back into society. We receive gifts in boxes
from stores that went out of business twenty years ago.

Erma Bombeck

Let me not forget that I am the daughter of a woman…
who herself never ceased to flower, untiringly,
during three quarters of a century.

Colette

Children and mothers never truly part—
Bound in the beating of each other's heart.

Charlotte Gray

> I prayed for this child, and the LORD
> has granted me what I asked of him.
>
> ♡
>
> **Hannah (1 Samuel 1:27)**

Special Moms

There are many ways to become a mom. Birthing a child is just one of them. Adopting a child is another. My husband and I have three children. Two of them are adopted, but as George Burns said regarding his adopted child, we can't remember which ones.

People who haven't adopted children can't fathom the maternal and paternal feelings an adoptive parent can have.

There are many ways to become a mom.

In our hearts there is no difference between our adopted children and our biological child. All three are our children, loved and believed in equally. Adoptive parents know exactly what I'm talking about. From the moment that child is placed in your arms, he or she is your own. You hurt when he hurts, you cheer for her accomplishments in life, and you're ready to protect that child from anyone who might not have his or her best interest at heart. You never forget that your son or daughter is a gift from God, emotionally connected to you from the moment you first started praying for a child of your own—which is often a lot longer than nine months.

> *Whoever welcomes a little child like*
> *this in my name welcomes me.*
> —Matthew 18:5

The Gift of Life

I didn't give you the gift of life,
But in my heart I know.
The love I feel is deep and real,
As if it had been so.

For us to have each other
Is like a dream come true!
No, I didn't give you the gift of life,
Life gave me the gift of you.

Anonymous

Somehow destiny comes into play.
These children end up with you and
you end up with them.
It's something quite magical.

Nicole Kidman, adoptive parent

Not flesh of my flesh
Nor bone of my bone,
But still miraculously my own.
Never forget for a single minute,
You didn't grow under my heart—but in it.

Fleur Conkling Heylinger

I feel that in the Heavens above,
The angels, whispering to one another,
Can find, among their burning terms of love,
None so devotional as that of "Mother."

Edgar Allan Poe

A mom's workplace never closes.

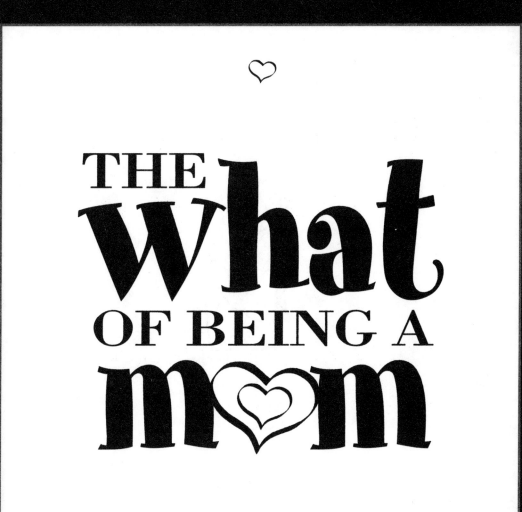

THE what OF BEING A mom

A mother's embrace is like a full-body bandage.

> There is no velvet so soft as a mother's lap,
> no rose as lovely as her smile, no path so flowery
> as that imprinted with her footsteps.

♡

Archibald Thompson

Mom Therapy

Modern technology has developed some of the softest fabrics ever to hit the market. Just feel your way through the stuffed animal collection of any toy store, and you'll see what I mean. They didn't have fabric that soft when we were young. Our stuffed animals were coarser, stiffer, and not nearly as cuddly as what's available today. It's a great time to be a baby!

But even the softest fabric is no match for the softness of a mother's embrace. Little else can duplicate the comfort it brings. Whether it's a scraped knee, a bad haircut, or a bruised spirit from one of life's unexpected tragedies, there's something about being nestled in your mother's arms that is healing to both your body and your emotions. A mother's embrace is like a full-body bandage that can envelop you and all your troubles in one fell swoop.

You might still have to carry your burdens, but while you're in Mom's arms, they just don't feel as heavy. And unlike a therapist who sets a timer and makes you leave just when you're starting to feel good again,

Mother's arms don't come with a timer. You can stay cradled there for as long as you want. You can stay until you're fully healed, or at least until the desire to get up and try again overrides the memory of your pain.

A teddy bear or a bear hug from Mom—they're both soft, they're both cuddly; but only one won't embarrass a grown man.

Even a grown boy needs his mother's hugs.

**Mother is the bank
where we deposit
all our hurts and worries.**

♡

Anonymous

Mother's arms are made of tenderness,
And sweet sleep blesses the child who lies therein.

♥

Victor Hugo

Blessed are the mothers of the earth.
They combine the practical and the spiritual
into the workable ways of human life.

♥

William L. Stinger

Mom Medicine

Mom's chicken soup is better than a miracle drug.

AND IT'S ALREADY FDA APPROVED.

Mom's smile can brighten your day faster than the most heralded antidepressant on the market–

WITHOUT THE SIDE EFFECTS.

**Mom's arms can rock
you to sleep
faster than any
sleeping pill.**

AND AFTERWARD,

YOU CAN STILL DRIVE AND OPERATE HEAVY MACHINERY.

Mom's TLC does more to speed healing than Vitamins E, D, or C.

AND IT DOESN'T HAVE

AN EXPIRATION DATE.

Mom's hug is better than an hour of therapy.

AND IT'S FREE.

Making the decision to have a child–
it's momentous.
It is to decide forever to have your heart
go walking around outside your body.

♥ Elizabeth Stone ♥

Lessons Moms Learn from Children

As mothers we teach our children lots of things. But they've taught us a few things too. Thanks to our children, we've learned that...

Tennis balls don't flush.

Spaghetti can double
as a hat.

It takes a whole package
of disposable razors to shave a dog.

VCRs don't play pizza.

Gum and hair are not easily parted.

Homework is not a coaster.

It takes a long time for a dog to lick a jarful of honey off itself.

A nasal cavity is not a good home for an olive.

Vacuum cleaners won't suck up a Slinky.

Some Chia pets grow naturally under a child's bed.

The most priceless works
of art in a home are those
drawn in crayon.

The commonest fallacy among women is that simply having children
makes them a mother—which is as absurd
as believing that having a piano makes one a musician.

♥

Sidney J. Harris

Motherhood brings as much joy as ever, but it still brings boredom,
exhaustion, and sorrow too. Nothing else ever will make you
as happy or as sad, as proud or as tired,
for nothing is quite as hard as helping a person develop
his own individuality especially while you struggle to keep your own.

♥

Marguerite Kelly and Elia Parsons

Songs for Moms

To All the Kids I've Bathed Before

On the Road Again (and again and again…)

Walking the Floor over You
(Did you forget your curfew?)

Like a Bridge over Dirty Laundry

The strength of motherhood is greater than natural laws.

♡

Barbara Kingsolver

Mom Muscles

Gold-medal Olympians, professional wrestlers, bodybuilders, lumberjacks—they may look strong, but they have nothing on a mother. Mothers are the strongest people on the face of the earth.

Mothers have been known to miraculously lift automobiles off an injured child. Eyewitnesses have reported seeing them run at lightning speed to reach an electrical plug before a two-year-old. These superhuman feats, accomplished without formal training or coaching, are what set mothers apart from the rest of us.

A mother's most incredible show of strength, however, has got to be lifting a diaper bag fifty times a day. Dads do it, too, but you can hear

Mothers are the strongest people on the face of the earth.

their groans from miles away. A mom just does it, effortlessly and without any warmup whatsoever. Let's see Arnold Schwarzenegger compete with that!

So why haven't we seen a mom featured on the cover of a box of Wheaties? Why isn't there a Diaper Bag Lifting event in the Olympics? Good questions. Maybe it's just a matter of time.

**Mother's love is peace.
It need not be acquired,
it need not be deserved.**

Erich Fromm

No language can express the power
and beauty and heroism of a mother's love.

Edwin H. Chapin

A mother understands
what a child does not say.

Jewish Proverb

Sooner or later we all quote our mothers.

Bern Williams

Never have more children than you have car windows.

Erma Bombeck

Mom-isms

"Shut that door! Are you trying to air-condition the whole neighborhood?"

"That perm looks fine. In fact, it looks downright electrifying!"

"Don't make me pull this car over!"

"Do I look like
a maid?"

"One of these days, I'm not
going to be around."

"...And don't give me any of your
'I dropped my sandwich on the floor
and the dog ate it' excuses!"

"Keep going and you're
going to break that."

"No playing ball in the house."

No matter how perfect
your mother thinks you are,
she will always want to fix your hair.

Suzanne Beilenson

Moms always make room for their children.

THE **when** OF BEING A m♥m

The joys of motherhood are never fully experienced until the children are in bed.

♡

Anonymous

A man's work is from sun to sun,
but a mother's work is never done.

Anonymous

It's All in the Timing

When does a mother love? When the report card being handed to her is filled with As? When the dishes are done, the grass is mowed, the trash is taken out, the beds are made, and the phone is back on the hook?

Mothers love 24/7, in the good times and the bad. Friends will sometimes put a limit on their love. But not a mom. Mom hangs in there. She believes in her child when the child doesn't even believe in him- or herself. A mom's love knows no limits.

Mothers love 24/7.

A father may turn his back on his child;

brothers and sisters may become inveterate enemies;

husbands may desert their wives and wives their husbands.

But a mother's love endures through all; in good repute,

in bad repute, in the face of the world's condemnation,

a mother still loves on.

♥ Washington Irving ♥

No matter how old a mother is,
she watches her middle-aged children
for signs of improvement.

Florida Scott-Maxwell

By and large, mothers and housewives
are the only workers who do not have regular time off.
They are the great vacationless class.

Anne Morrow Lindbergh

Her children arise up,
and call her blessed.

—Proverbs 31:28 KJV

Life began with waking up and loving my mother's face.

♡

George Eliot

All Rise!

The scripture on the opposite page is amazing. But not because this woman's children call her blessed. That's touching, yes, but what's amazing is that this wonderful woman somehow gets her children to *rise up* and do it! Now, how does she accomplish that little feat?

The scripture doesn't say that this mom has to keep going into her kids' bedrooms a half-dozen times, trying to get them to wake up so they can call her blessed. It says they do it all on their own! They just rise up and say, "Mom, you're blessed!" No one has to drag them out of bed, and they don't hit the snooze alarm six times before doing it. They're not even trying to sweet-talk their way into borrowing the family chariot for the night. They simply want to honor their mom by calling her blessed, and they're so moved by her goodness that they even rise up to do it. First thing in the morning, before their Honey Nut Cheerios, before they finish the homework assignment that was supposed to be done the night before, before they complain about not being able to get into the bathroom because their sister is hogging it…before all that, these kids pause long enough to call their mother blessed.

Kinda brings a tear to your eye, doesn't it?

"You're blessed!"

A Mother Gets Her Wings

There are certain times when a mom earns her title more than others:

parent-teacher meetings the week of report cards

stomach-flu season

teething

the junior-high years

sleepovers

the practicing of any large musical instrument— especially bagpipes or drums

shopping with a three-year-old

They always looked back before turning the corner,
for their mother was always at the window, to nod, and smile,
and wave her hand at them. Somehow it seemed as if
they couldn't have got through the day without that,
for whatever their mood might be, the last glimpse
of that motherly face was sure to affect them like sunshine.

❤ Louisa May Alcott ❤

**A mother holds her children's hands for a while,
but their hearts forever.**

Anonymous

A High-Flying Act

I love the circus. Who doesn't? The dancing bears, the clowns, and the sword swallowers all make for an entertaining show. (Although I don't understand why the sword swallowers can't just cut their food before they eat!)

Without a doubt, my favorite act is the flying trapeze artists. It's incredible to watch these skilled athletes spin through the air one, two, even three times and still manage to connect with the hands of the catcher with precision timing.

As impressive as their performance is, though, these artists have the assurance of a safety net. They may not need the net until they're ready to dismount, but it must be comforting for them to know it's there. The net must be one of the reasons they dare to attempt greater and greater feats.

In a lot of ways, our moms are our safety nets. They want us to soar. They want us to have our independence, and they'll happily cheer us on to greater and greater accomplishments. But they can also be counted on to be there in case we fall, just like the net is there for the trapeze artist—ready when needed, but always just outside of the limelight. Moms know that the real show is in the flying.

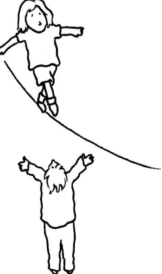

Moms are like a safety net.

Words from Moms throughout History

Mona Lisa's mother: After all that money your father and I spent on braces, that's the biggest smile you can give us?

Columbus's mother: I don't care what you've discovered, you still could have written!

Michelangelo's mother: Can't you draw on walls like other children? Do you have any idea how hard it is to get that paint off the ceiling?

Napoleon's mother: All right, if you aren't hiding your report card inside your jacket, take your hand out of there and show me!

Abraham Lincoln's mother: Again with the stovepipe hat, Abe? Can't you just wear a baseball cap like the other kids?

Mary's mother: I'm not upset that your lamb followed you to school, Mary, but I would like to know how he got a better grade than you.

SCRITCH
SCRATCH

Albert Einstein's mother: But it's your senior picture, Al. Can't you do something about your hair? Styling gel, mousse, *something?*

Thomas Edison's mother: Of course I'm proud that you invented the electric light bulb, son. Now turn it off and get to sleep!

Paul Revere's mother: I don't care where you think you have to go, young man, midnight is past your bedtime!

Superman's mother: Clark, your father and I have discussed it, and we've decided you can have your own telephone line. Now will you quit spending so much time in all those phone booths?

Humpty Dumpty's mother:

Humpty, if I've told you once, I've told you a hundred times not to sit on that wall. But would you listen to me? Nooooo!

Jonah's mother: That's a nice story. Now tell me where you've really been for the last three days.

Life is not measured by the number of breaths you take, but by the moments that take your breath away.

♡

Anonymous

Moments

A mom never forgets the moment she became a mother. The moment she first cradled that little one in her arms or held that toddler or hugged that adolescent, she knew it was a moment to lock away in her memory forever. It's a moment that comes back to her when her son or daughter graduates from high school, walks down the wedding aisle, or holds his or her own baby for the first time. Motherhood is about moments.

A mom never forgets the moment she became a mother.

Before you were conceived I wanted you.
Before you were born I loved you. Before you were here an hour
I would die for you. This is the miracle of life.

Maureen Hawkins

In the sheltered simplicity of the first days after a baby is born,
one sees again the magical closed circle.
The miraculous sense of two people existing for each other.

Anne Morrow Lindbergh

Everybody today seems to be in such a terrible rush, anxious for greater
developments and greater riches and so on, so that children
have very little time for their parents. Parents have very little time
for each other, and in the home begins the disruption of peace of the world.

Mother Teresa

I Saw Tomorrow

I saw tomorrow marching by
On little children's feet;
Within their forms and faces read
Her prophecy complete.
I saw tomorrow look at me
From little children's eyes,
And thought how carefully we'd teach
If we were really wise.

Anonymous

It will be gone before you know it.
The fingerprints on the wall appear
higher and higher.
Then suddenly they disappear.

Dorothy Evslin

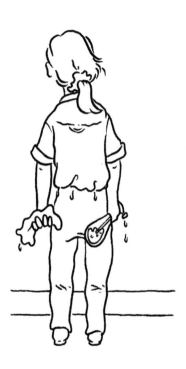

Moms are everywhere!

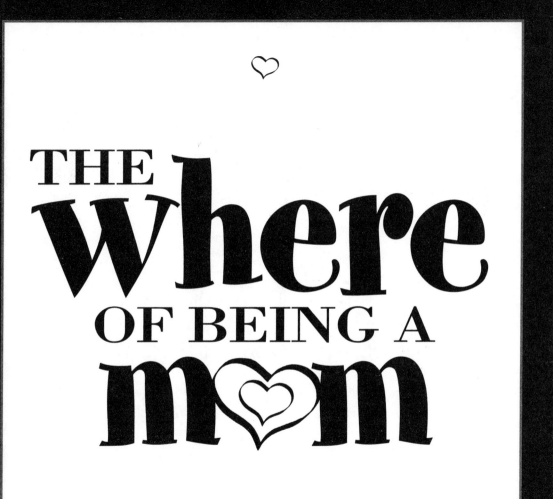

THE where OF BEING A m♡m

*Those yellowing pieces of paper and gallery-worthy crayon drawings
are a mom's prized possessions.*

A positive mom doesn't take away her children's troubles; she teaches them how to look for the hand of God in the midst of them.

♡

Karol Ladd

Hidden Treasures

They're in my attic. Boxes and boxes and boxes of them. They're from kindergarten, first grade, and all the way through high school. Tests, term papers, science projects, school-play costumes, priceless works of art—I've kept them all, tucked safely away there. Why? Because that's what moms do. Those yellowing pieces of paper and gallery-worthy crayon drawings are our prized possessions. No, we wouldn't get much for them on eBay, but to us they're more valuable than an original Van Gogh. Why? Because one look and they bring back emotion-filled memories of children whose youthful faces have long since been replaced by adult ones.

These one-of-a-kind treasures take us back to a magical place where giggles, cuddles, and chest-squeezing child hugs once melted our hearts and made all the troubles of our day go away. That plaster-of-Paris hand print presented by a wide-eyed, six-year-old child one Christmas; the macaroni necklace crafted by a four-year-old in Sunday school; the glitter-and-cotton-ball purse an eight-year-old surprised us with one Mother's Day—give up these masterpieces? Would anyone dare ask the Louvre to give up the *Mona Lisa?*

The photo ornament, the hand-painted plate, and any number of other beloved handmade gifts are our tickets for countless journeys back to a place where love, real and uncomplicated, is captured and frozen in time. They sit in the attic awaiting each visit. And even though someday we may be too old and weak to keep carting these treasures from house to house, old attic to new attic, we still don't have to let go of them. That's what professional movers are for.

You never realize how much your mother loves you
till you explore the attic—and find every letter you ever sent her,
every finger painting, clay pot, bead necklace,
Easter chicken, cardboard Santa Claus,
paper-lace Mother's Day card, and school report since day one.

♥ Pam Brown ♥

Moms in the Home

Neurotics build castles in the air,
psychotics live in them. My mother cleans them.

Rita Rudner

The instruction received at the mother's knee,…
together with the pious and sweet souvenirs of the fireside,
are never effaced entirely from the soul.

Abbe Hugo Felicite de Lamennais

My theory on housework is, if the item doesn't multiply,

smell, catch fire, or block the refrigerator door, let it be.

No one else cares. Why should you?

♥

Erma Bombeck

Moms in the Kitchen

All the philosophy in our house is not in the study. A good deal
is in the kitchen, where a fine old lady thinks high thoughts
and does good deeds while she cooks and scrubs.

Louisa May Alcott

My mother's menu consisted of two choices:
Take it or leave it.

Buddy Hackett

The most remarkable thing about my mother is that for thirty years
she served the family nothing but leftovers.
The original meal has never been found.

Calvin Trillin

O Mother, Where Art Thou?

3:00 A.M.   Feed and change baby.

3:15 A.M.   Play with now wide-awake baby.

4:00 A.M.   Fall back asleep with baby in rocking chair.

4:28 A.M.   Wake up and put sleeping baby in crib. Go back to bed.

4:30 A.M.   Get glass of water for toddler who just stumbled into the room.

4:40 A.M.   Fall back asleep.

4:50 A.M.   Baby cries again.

4:51 A.M.   Open right eye.

4:52 A.M.   Open left eye.

4:53 A.M.   Get up, feed and change baby.

5:10 A.M.   Fall back asleep.

5:45 A.M.   Alarm clock goes off. Hit snooze alarm.

5:55 A.M.   Hit snooze alarm.

6:05 A.M.   Hit snooze alarm.

6:15 A.M.   Hit alarm clock.

6:25 A.M.   Hit wall with alarm clock

7:15 A.M.   Oversleep. Wake up. Have only forty-five minutes to get eight-year-old and twelve-year-old to their schools.

7:16 A.M.   Wake up eight-year-old and twelve-year-old.

7:18 A.M.   Wake up eight-year-old and twelve-year-old.

7:28 A.M.   Repeat above.

       7:30 A.M.   Pack lunches.

       7:35 A.M.   Kiss husband good-bye.

7:40 A.M.   Load baby and toddler into car and drive eight-year-old and twelve-year-old to school.

8:05 A.M.   Stop by drugstore to buy diapers.

10:30 A.M.   Take baby to pediatrician for three-month checkup.

2:00 P.M.	Take toddler to dentist.
2:50 P.M.	Pick up eight-year-old from school.
3:05 P.M.	Pick up twelve-year-old from school.
3:30 P.M.	Drop off twelve-year-old at park for baseball practice.
3:45 P.M.	Drop off eight-year-old at piano lessons.
4:20 P.M.	Handle phone call from church committee leader asking for volunteers. She explains that they need moms to volunteer because they can't ask those who have "real" jobs.

4:30 P.M.	Pick up twelve-year-old at park.
4:45 P.M.	Pick up eight-year-old from piano lessons.
5:00 P.M.	People with just one "real" job are now clocking out and calling it a day. Wonder what that feels like.
5:10 P.M.	Make dinner.
6:00 P.M.	Eat dinner.
7:00 P.M.	Help kids with their homework.

8:00 P.M.	Bathe baby and toddler.
8:30 P.M.	Put baby and toddler to bed.
9:00 P.M.	Put eight- and twelve-year-olds to bed.
10:45 P.M.	Breathe. Ah…there's finally time for it!

**There was never a child so lovely
but his mother was glad to get him asleep.**

Ralph Waldo Emerson

My kids always perceived the bathroom
as a place where you wait it out
until all the groceries are unloaded from the car.

Erma Bombeck

Motherhood:
All love begins and ends there.

Robert Browning

The influence of moms can change the world.

THE why OF BEING A m♥m

Moms are gifted unravelers.

A mother is neither cocky nor proud because she knows the school principal may call at any minute to report that her child has just driven a motorcycle through the gymnasium.

♡

Mary Kay Blakely

There's Something about Mom

Why do we need moms? Because we need someone to whom we can go for a reassuring hug when our knees—or our self-esteem—get a little bruised. We need someone we can call when our lives get tangled up. Moms are gifted unravelers.

We need the memories moms provide—memories that will long outlive them and will bring us comfort all the days of our lives, just like the memories of their mothers gave them comfort.

We need our mothers' faith, because knowing someone believes in you and sees your worth usually makes you live up to it. We need a mother's concern, for it's reassuring to know that someone cares about our safety.

God knew we would need this special lady in our lives—that's why He assigned one to each of us. It doesn't matter whether yours is a birth mom, adopted mom, or just someone in your life who has become your "mom." You know all the reasons she's so special to you. And that's all that matters.

God knew we would need this special lady.

**One of the oldest human needs
is having someone to wonder where you are
when you don't come home at night.**

Margaret Mead

Moms Matter

No influence is so powerful as that of the mother.

♥

Sarah Josepha Hale

An ounce of mother is worth a pound of clergy.

♥

Spanish proverb

**Children are likely to live up
to what you believe of them.**

♡

Lady Bird Johnson

Moms Impact the Future

A mom can't see the future, but she can raise children with enough faith to handle whatever it holds.

A mom doesn't have all the answers, but she can raise a child who is inquisitive enough to help in the search for a few of them.

A mom can't single-handedly change the world, but if every mom made a positive impact on her own children's lives, and those children grew up to make a positive impact on their children's lives, and so on, eventually the world would have to change.

The Sculptor's Opportunity

I took a piece of common clay
And idly fashioned it one day.
And as my fingers pressed it, still
It moved and yielded to my will.
I came again when days were past;
The bit of clay was hard at last.
The form I gave it still it bore,
And I could fashion it no more!
I took a piece of living clay,
And gently pressed it day by day,
And moulded with my power and art
A young child's soft and yielding heart.
I came again when years had gone;
It was a man I looked upon.
He still that early impress bore,
And I could fashion it no more!

Anonymous

God Says It's Important

*"Honor your father and mother"—which is
the first commandment with a promise—"that it may go well
with you and that you may enjoy long life on the earth."*
—Ephesians 6:2–3

At age thirty-three, Jesus was well into adulthood—yet He loved and cared for His mother. While on the cross, He took the time to make sure the woman He called Mom would be taken care of.

*He said…to the disciple, "Here is your mother."
From that time on, this disciple
took her into his home.*
—John 19:26–27

Too Good to Be Forgotten

A mother's love is indeed the golden link that binds youth to age;
and he is still but a child, however time may have
furrowed his cheek, or silvered his brow, who can yet recall,
with a softened heart, the fond devotion or the gentle chidings
of the best friend that God ever gives us.

❤

Bovee

Of all the rights of women,
the greatest is to be a mother.

❤

Lin Yutang

**Of course I'd like to be the ideal mother.
But I'm too busy raising children.**

Mommy ("Family Circus," by Bil Keane)

The Perfect Mom

A mom isn't a good mom if her children are perfect. She's a good mom if her children know that even failure won't change her love for them.

A mom isn't a good mom if her children make it to the top of the ladder. She's a good mom if, on whatever rung of the ladder they land, they didn't get there by stepping on others.

A mom isn't a good mom if her children win the gold at the Olympics. She's a good mom if her children have enough faith to win the gold in life.

*Moms love—
no matter what!*

Moms grow sharing hearts.

A mom isn't a good mom if her children are on the honor roll. She's a good mom if her children have honorable hearts.

A mom isn't a good mom if her children make the cover of a national magazine. She's a good mom if her children have enough confidence to make others feel special.

A mom isn't a good mom if her children grow up to someday lead a country. She's a good mom if her children grow up to appreciate the cost of freedom.

A mom isn't a good mom simply because of her children's

Moms instill strength of character.

*Moms encourage
the pursuit of dreams.*

external accomplishments. She's a good mom when their internal strength of character can't help but shine through.

A mom isn't a good mom if her children become what she wants them to become. She's a good mom if they know they're free to pursue their dreams and God's plan for their lives, and that they only have control over the pursuit, not the outcome.

*The future belongs to those
who believe in the beauty of their dreams.*

♡

Eleanor Roosevelt

Prayer is one of the best ways to show a mother's love.

THE
how
OF BEING A
mom

You don't need a lot of money to raise a great kid.

A rich child often sits in a poor mother's lap.

♡

Danish Proverb

Mother's How-To

There is no one set of rules for mothering. Some parents who are stricter than others think their way is the right way. Others who emphasize encouragement and freedom feel their style is right. Some moms think homeschooling is best; others believe public or private schools offer advantages.

Some children who have been raised in strict homes grow up and have problems. Some children who have been raised in lenient homes grow up and have problems. Poor parents have raised presidents and doctors; rich parents have raised presidents and doctors. Uneducated parents have raised Harvard graduates, and some highly educated parents have watched their children drop out of school.

The "right way" is probably somewhere in the middle of all these extremes. Mothers need to be strict, but they also need to be flexible. We need to be encouragers, but we also need to set boundaries. And still, no one method will result in perfect young people. Why? Each child is different. Each situation is different. And each parent is different. The only thing that is sure to have a positive effect is a mother's unconditional love.

**Before becoming a mother
I had a hundred theories
on how to bring up children.
Now I have seven children
and only one theory: Love them,
especially when they least deserve to be loved.**

Kate Samperi

True mothers have to be made of steel to withstand the difficulties that are sure to beset their children.

♡

Rachel Billington

How to Make a Mom

It's easy to make a mom. All you need are…

2 **arms** of steel for carrying the family's jackets, sodas, camera, and souvenirs at amusement parks.

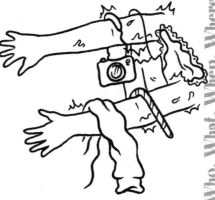

2 **legs** of iron for the 268,495 steps she'll take each day chasing the two-year-old.

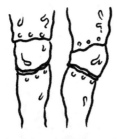

2 flexible but sturdy **feet,** capable of moving in all directions simultaneously. (The right one should also have the strength and durability to press down on a gas pedal for hours on end, because so much of her life is spent in a car.)

2 multifunctional **hands,** absorbent enough to wipe away tears but strong enough to help another human being stand until they have enough strength to do it on their own.

1 **tongue,** capable of both correction and love, usually simultaneously.

1 **lap,** soft enough to provide comfort but sturdy enough to offer the protection of a fortress.

2 **shoulders** to cry on when hurting and to lean on when the child has lost his or her footing.

2 **eyes** with **x-ray vision,** capable of seeing through the most inventive excuse for getting home late.

Multiple **double joints** are also required, because the ideal mother is also a contortionist who can twist her body into amazingly inhuman shapes as she reaches from the driver's seat of an automobile to separate the three children wrestling in the backseat, all while not taking her eyes off the road for a second.

Bionic hearing is an absolute must. Since the beginning of time moms have had the ability to hear everything. You don't even have to speak it, and they'll hear it. They know what you're thinking, they know what you're planning, and they know what your teacher wrote in the note you're hiding in your pocket.

Of course, you can't build a mom without that one **last nerve**. This is very important in the construction of a mother. The nerve is small, but it must be strong because so many people end up getting on it.

And finally, moms need **a good heart**. One that loves unreservedly, unselfishly, and unconditionally. A mother's love is second only to God's love.

The process of shaping the child...shapes also the mother herself.
Reverence for her sacred burden calls her to all that is pure
and good, that she may teach primarily
by her own humble, daily example.

Elisabeth Elliot

How Do They Do It?

Mothers Know

My sister said once: "Anything I don't want Mother to know,

I don't even think of, if she's in the room."

♥

Agatha Christie

Mothers Dream

A mother is someone who dreams great dreams for you,

but then she lets you chase the dreams

you have for yourself and loves you just the same.

Anonymous

Mothers Teach

The mother is and must be, whether she knows it

or not, the greatest, strongest and most lasting

teacher her children have.

Hannah Whitall Smith

Mothers Heal

Who ran to help me when I fell,
And would some pretty story tell,
Or kiss the place to make it well?
My Mother.

Jane Taylor

Mothers Show

My mother is a woman
who speaks with her life
as much as her tongue.

Kesaya E. Noder

Mothers Pray

I remember my mother's prayers and they have always followed me.

They have clung to me all my life.

Abraham Lincoln

Mothers Hope

Youth fades; love droops,

the leaves of friendships fall;

A mother's secret hope

outlives them all.

Oliver Wendell Holmes

Mothers Advise

When your mother asks, "Do you want a piece of advice?"

it is a mere formality. It doesn't matter if you answer yes or no.

You're going to get it anyway.

Erma Bombeck

Mothers Believe

A mother's love perceives no impossibilities.

Paddock

Mothers Sacrifice

A mother is a person who, seeing there are only four pieces of pie for five

people, promptly announces she never did care for pie.

Tenneva Jordan

Mothers Support

There was a hemlock tree on the west side of the property.

That was the tree I used to climb. The neighbors used to call to Mother,

"Kit! Kathy is in the top of the hemlock!"

"Yes, I know. Don't scare her. She doesn't know it's dangerous."

Katharine Hepburn

Mothers Encourage

Mama exhorted her children at every opportunity to "jump at de sun." We might not land on the sun, but at least we would get off the ground.

Zora Neale Hurston

Mothers Enrich

In search of my mother's garden, I found my own.

Alice Walker

Mothers Forgive

The heart of a mother is a deep abyss at the bottom of which you will always find forgiveness.

Honoré de Balzac

Mothers Love

All mothers are rich when they love their children.

There are no poor mothers, no ugly ones, no old ones.

Their love is always the most beautiful of joys.

Maurice Maeterlinck

Mothers Embolden

Mother love is the fuel that enables a normal

human being to do the impossible.

Anonymous

WHIMPER

Mothers Defend

A mother's love for her child is like nothing else in the world.

It knows no law, no pity; it dares all things

and crushes down remorselessly all that stands in its path.

Agatha Christie

Mothers Stay

Mother is the one we count on for the things that matter most of all.

♥

Katherine Butler Hathaway

> **Any mother could perform the jobs of several air-traffic controllers with ease.**
>
> Lisa Alther

'Taint Easy

Since babies don't come with instruction manuals chained to their ankles, mothering is mostly guesswork. A new mom can get plenty of advice from other, more experienced mothers, and there are plenty of parenting books on the market to help. But it's still up to each mom to chart her own course. She may choose to model certain qualities she sees in this mom, other qualities she sees in that mom, and so on, but her parenting style will ultimately be her own. Even when she tries her best to make all the right decisions, she's going to make some mistakes. It's inevitable. Even Mary lost track of Jesus when He slipped off to the temple to speak with the religious scholars of His day.

So do we throw in the towel and give up, citing the impossibility of our task? Absolutely not! (Besides, that'll just add one more towel to the laundry.) All we can do is the best job we can, and keep reminding ourselves how quickly the childhood years pass. Before we know it, our children will be grown and facing their own parenting challenges.

Even Mary lost track of Jesus.

Remember the song "Sunrise, Sunset" from the Broadway musical *Fiddler on the Roof?* It's about the speed of passing childhoods. One day we're carrying our children in our arms; the next day they're grown adults helping us across the street. No matter how much we'd like to slow down the process, we can't. Time doesn't stop for any of us, regardless of what fun we're having. The years between *"Wah!"* and "Where are the car keys?" are few and fleeting. All we can do is try to find a little laughter in the midst of those nose-wiping, diaper-changing, milk-spilling, toy-flushing, music-blaring, report-card-hiding, tattoo-debating, biker-dating, praying-they-graduate days. Nothing lasts forever—and that's especially true of childhood.

*Nothing lasts forever
—especially childhood.*

**My mother had a great deal of trouble with me,
but I think she enjoyed it.**

Mark Twain

Moms are the best!

The Last Word on Being a Mom

Many moms like to have the last word, but this time, we're having it. The last word about mothers is the same word we started with—where would any of us be without them?

So whether you have a job outside the home in addition to being a full-time mom or you're a stay-at-home full-time mom, whether you're known as Mom, Mother, Madre, Ma, Mother-in-Law, or any other title you may have chosen, just know that you are loved. And appreciated. We thank you for always being there for us...

**when we're acting our worst
when we need an unconditional friend
when we have nowhere else to turn
when we can't see our worth
when we've lost our direction
when we need a helping hand
when we want to feel unconditionally, unashamedly,
and unmeasurably loved.**

That's what moms do!

Mother Proverbs

Better to be safe than to walk into a teenager's closet without a hard hat.

The pen is mightier than the laundry detergent.

Where there's smoke, there's a hair dryer, a curling iron, an electric shaver, and a hot lather machine all plugged into the same outlet.

A penny saved from the vacuum cleaner is a vacuum cleaner that still works.

Purple Heart for Moms

Awarded to

_____

Mother of

_____

On this day of

_____

For Exceptional Bravery in the Line of Duty
Injury sustained on

_____

Check all that apply:

❏ Tripped over skateboard

❏ Injured during child's science-project explosion

❏ Endured severe gastrointestinal pain and discomfort after eating
twelve boxes of fund-raising chocolate bars for child's school

- ❑ Severe Hula Hoop entanglement (Last words heard before the incident were "Here, let me show you how it's done!")
- ❑ Right foot muscle cramps brought on by pressing on gas and brake pedals for extended periods of time, going above and beyond the call of taxi duty
- ❑ Carpal tunnel syndrome from wrapping Christmas gifts until dawn on Christmas Eve
- ❑ Wrenched back while playing Twister at nine-year-old's birthday party (Some configurations should not be attempted by anyone over the age of thirty.)
- ❑ Other: _____

Signature _____

Witness _____

Date _____

One New Dress

Bearer will receive one new dress, selected by your offspring. (Remember that bunny outfit you made me wear one Easter, Mom? It's payback time. Let's go shopping!)

Hot Meal Pass

Bearer is entitled to one hot meal. Family members will get their own salt and pepper, extra napkins, and beverage refills while Mom gets to actually eat her meal before it gets cold.

Free Pass

Bearer will receive one pass through the house without having to walk on a single piece of dirty laundry left lying on the floor.

One Takeout Dinner

Bearer is entitled to order one takeout meal for dinner—without having to make any side dishes or provide beverages to go along with it. Plastic utensils will also be provided.

Hairstyling Session

Bearer is entitled to one appointment with the hairstylist of your choice, with the solemn promise that this will not be a reenactment of the permanent YOU gave

_____ in junior-high school.
[fill in name]

One Day Trip

Bearer is entitled to one day trip—destination of her choice. (Tripping over a toy left in the middle of the living room doesn't qualify.)

Motorized Therapy Session

Bearer is entitled to one relaxing, scenic drive—without having to pick up anyone along the way or take anyone anywhere for anything.

Free Pass

Bearer is entitled to one free pass on a sink-load of dishes.
(You've got all day tomorrow to do them.)

Talk Time

Bearer is entitled to one hour of uninterrupted telephone usage, no matter who's trying to get through on Call Waiting.

Neck and Shoulder Massage

Bearer is entitled to one free massage, lasting between five seconds and five days, depending on the stress level endured that week.

Foot Massage

Bearer is entitled to one free foot massage.
(Stepping on a bathroom scale with an electrical short doesn't count.)

Silent Night

Bearer is entitled to one evening without any complaining or arguing from a single one of your offspring.

Mom, you are special. You are amazing. You are loved.